MW01603035

Hom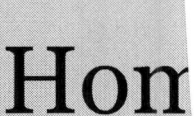g

poetry & prose

Stefanie Briar

@stefanie.briar.poetry

Copyright © 2021 by Stefanie Briar.

All rights reserved.

This book or any portion thereof my not be reproduced or used in any manner whatsoever without the express written permission of the publisher except for the use of brief quotations in a book review.

ISBN: 9798693470910

Instagram:

@stefanie.briar.poetry

Publication Date: 1/1/2021

First Printing: 2021

Kindle Direct Publishing

Cover Design by: Kaitlin Coppock

Cover Art and Chapter Sketches by: Rebecca Connell
@rebecca_anniee

Journal page illustrations by: Kalyani Datta

@kalyaniidatta

For my Avalon:

May you grow to be kind and strong.

May you take this world by storm.

May you believe and delight in your own power.

And when you ever doubt it...

I will remind you. As long as I live.

In loving memory of my father:

You taught me to love words before I knew sentences.

You believed in me long before I did.

Now, in your absence, I live loudly enough

(and cause enough trouble)

for the both of us.

To my chosen family: I love you all until the stars burn out.

This is your raised fist, your "Enough of this!"

This is you *reclaiming* your p o w e r.

This is you owning your journey;

This is your *healing*.

This is your <u>homecoming</u>.

W e l c o m e

back

to

Y

O

U.

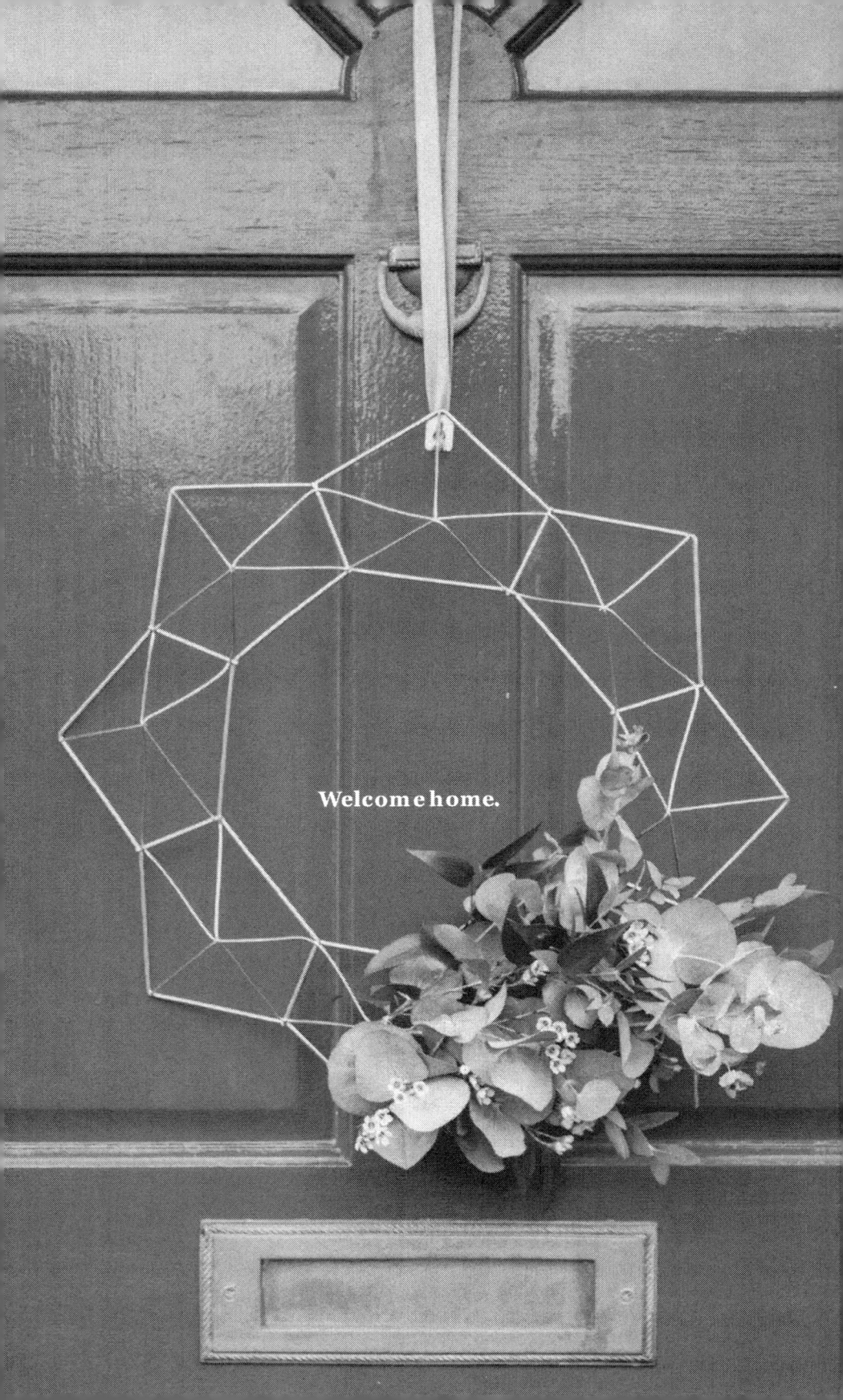

Welcome home.

Table of Contents

You Are Never Too Far Gone: Poetry

Break the Chains - 14

Free - 16

Homecoming - 18/19

Rebuilding - 20

The Million Dollar Question - 22

Clean - 24

Do Not Let the Clock Run Out - 26/27

The Architect - 28/29

From Half-Baked to Awake - 30/31

Bloom - 33

To You, From You - 34/35

Brightest Self -36

She Was Free - 38

Choosing You - 40

Memories - 41

The Tide Turns - 42

In My Tomorrows - 44

Each Day Since - 46/47

Back in Bloom - 48

Value - 50

PhotosyntheSIS - 51

Lost and Bound - 53

Self-Suture - 54

The Broken One - 55

Unbroken - 57

Misplaced Apologies - 58

A New Frequency - 59

Closure - 60

Paradox - 62

Stay Away - 63

If Love Wasn't Blind - 64/65

Essence - 66/67

Mirror, Mirror - 68

I Will Be Here - 70

Heavy is the Head - 72-75

Baggage Claim - 77

I See You - 78/79

Change - 81

Echo - 82/83

Nothings - 84/85

Sediment - 86

When I Lose Myself - 88

The Tree - 89

Meant for More - 91

Fire & Rain - 92

Anxiety - 93

Fairweather Flickers - 94/95

Picking up A Pen - 96

Dear - 97

Sacred - 98

The Right - 99

I Choose Truth - 101

I Will Wait - 103

Lasting Love - 104

Lesson Learned, Wisdom Earned - 106/107

Your Arrow - 108

Poetry - 110

The Audacity - 111

Wreckless - 112

I've Got Me - 114

Quiet of the Night - 115

Table for One - 116

Grand Crescendo - 118

I Kept the Words - 119

The Art of Rising – 121

Until the Day - 122

Rainbow - 124/125

You Can Always Come Home: Prose

Love Multiplies - 128

Not Yours - 129

Rare Heart - 131

A Link Remains - 132

Quiet Survival - 134

Some Days - 135

Feather - 136

The Healing Garden - 138/139

The Path - 140

Porch Light - 141

Let Your Axis Tilt - 142

Phoenix - 144

Wanderlust - 145

You Can Always Come Home - 146

First? You. - 147

Letting Go - 148

Wounded - 150

Set Free - 151

Amethyst Heart - 152

My Own Company - 154

Diamond Mine - 155

Turn it Around - 156

Sleep Soundly - 157

Still Here - 159

Thank You - 160

Glow-Up - 161

Unsaid Apology - 162

Comeback - 164

Nothing More, Nothing less - 165

In Time - 166

Grief - 168

The Perfect Weapon - 170

Our Hearts - 171

Voices - 172

What Brings You Joy - 173

So Much More - 174

Too Much - 176

Only Human - 177

Well-Versed - 178

Breathe - 180

Monsters - 182

Anchors - 183

You Will Not Stay Lost - 185

Self-Love - 186

Brokenness - 188

Stillness - 190

Knock – 191

Hurricane - 192

Born to Burn - 194

One Day, They Will Go Quiet - 195

I Used to - 196

Blowing Off Dust - 198

The Moment I Knew - 199

Dried Flowers - 200

I Am Coming In - 202

Calm Center - 204

Grand Gesture - 205

It Feels Like This - 206

Love, S.B. - 208/209

The Words Are Your Own: Journal - 212
Epilogue: "Chrysalis" - 224-229

You Are Never Too Far Gone

(Poetry)

I know you feel lost;

I know your mind falters...

unable to remember

the last time

you felt your own power.

But allow me to remind you

of one, simple truth...

You

are

s t i l l

Y

O

U;

And you will (in time),

-b-r-e-a-k- the c-h-a-i-n-s-

that *confine* you.

Break the Chains

"Free" never happens accidentally.

Find what brings you peace;
learn what *truly* makes you   h a p p y...

and then do it-
purposefully.

Free

Today,

as the light

b

r

e

a

k

s

I wake; eyes open

for the first time in a long time.

And I can't help but think

that today is a good day

to return home to myself.

And so, I smile-

strange; it's been a while.

It is time to remove the layers of dust

that built up

in the wake of the days

since you stopped being *m i n e.*

I pass the mirror;

I stare into the eyes of a stranger.

It's time she and I
got acquainted.

Over coffee
and stories,
that she stored in a pen,

through ink tears on paper,
she comes home again,
and draws the curtains.

A beat.
A breath.
A deep
s
i
g
h,
she lets in the sunlight,
and gazes out the window
at the rest
of her life.

Homecoming

I know what it's like
to be my own wrecking ball;
to drive it straight into my whole l i f e
and then lament the end result...

Broken pieces.

Broken people.

Broken dreams.

Broken *me*...

Broken everything.

But I also know how:

To fix.

To fuse.

To build.

To choose;

To bolster it back up again.
on an even stronger foundation

The from-ashes truth?
nothing is beyond r e p a i r.
Not. Even. You.

Rebuilding

When it comes to others

I

r

a

i

n

grace down like wine.

I hang the sun over their head,
and *force it to shine*.

So why isn't the same true
when the troubles are *mine*?

The Million Dollar Question

Instead of trying

To stop the

r

a

i

n,

I came to the conclusion

That it's not about

Getting wet...

It's about learning

To dance in it.

And in learning that?

I am *free;*

I am clean...

f i n a l l y.

Clean

If you ever need a   p u s h
to tell the truth,
to live out the *real* version of you;

Remember the passage of time,
and how it turns on a dime.

It is a giver,
and a taker.

It is *cruel* to hearts.
and *kind* to souls.
It   r e s i s t s   all attempts to control.

You have   e n o u g h   of it
until you have

n

o

n

e

of it.

Rather than fear it,
let it mold you like clay;
into something beautiful and brave.

Do   not   die

before being y o u.

do not let the clock run out

before you tell your truth.

You deserve better of you...

we

all

do.

Do Not Let the Clock Run Out

Stagnation...

I know it well;

I know how hours

c

o

l

l

a

p

s

e

behind soulless eyes,

staring years through walls;

so angry at everything

that may or may not

have done me wrong.

The problem,

as it turns out...

was ***m e*** all along.

I am no *victim of circumstance,*

but I am g u i l t y

of never giving myself a chance.

I am no great artist,

but I know how

to paint myself   i n v i s i b l e;

to pretend I don't belong,

and to drain the light from

every crack it count enter from.

I was the architect

of my own destruction

for

    so

       l o n g.

But instead of a brush,

I picked up a pen,

and I have not stopped since.

Real healing happens within.

All you ever really need to do

is begin.

The Architect

You spend all this time

half-baked; languishing

you feel like raw dough; raw material

not yet in your correct form.

You wait for someone (or something)

to come along

and turn you into a *finished product*.

You have been waiting

for the w r o n g set of hands

to make you into what you should be.

The helping hands you've ignored

(y o u r o w n)

have been waiting to be used all along;

to stir, shake, whisk, knead you

to all but *beat you into yourself*.

They wait-

for you

to claim your own light.

We alone have the power

to decide how we end up.

Your own light is the source

that will forge your molecules correctly,

and render you something

"just right"

(as "just right" as any of us can be).

This is your wake-up-call

if your toothpick didn't come out clean.

From "Half-Baked" to "Awake"

I bloom

from the spot

where I pulled you out of me

by the   r o o t s,

wishing I didn't have to choose

between my *sanity*

and an   o   p   e   n   *wound.*

But the rain has come,

and *closed me up.*

Now, I have

room to   g r o w.

Bloom

My skin,
my surface
is made of
c
   r
     a
       c
         k
           s

Where I store
everything I *lack*.

I try to close them;
stitch them through.

But they open anew,
bleeding; when I
don't want them to.

And so, I speak
life and love
over and into
my w o u n d s...

You're okay.

You're pretty.
Intelligently witty.

Your body is just fine,
and gets you from A to B.

Your eyes in the sunlight
are a sight to behold.

And you'd never hesitate
to help anyone.

How many times have I told you
that beauty lives
within your very skin;
your creative hands,
your fierce ways,
your future plans,
and your compassion?

34

You are so
L
    O
        V
           E
              D
by those who know you,
and your a n x i e t y
has not become you.

But you rationalize
your insecurities into -c-h-a-i-n-s-
and shackle them
to the *same old pain;*
Again.

And again.

And again....

Every time you forget
your own power,

You cower in corners
you force yourself into,
when your spirit
can fill *entire rooms*
without even t r y i n g to.

I will not stop
pouring love
into your -b-r-o-k-e-n- places,
until flowers bloom
from the *empty spaces.*

To; you.
From,
You.

To you, From you

35

I will shine a light

on your brightest self,

until the day

you can see it

for

y
o
u
r
s
e
l
f

Brightest Self

She finally opened

her s h a k i n g hands;

to let go

of what wasn't meant to be.

Imagine her surprise

when *she* was

s

e

t

f

r

e

e.

She Was Free

It is perfectly okay
to paint the sky g r e y,
and place white sheets
like shrouds; like clouds
over what once made you happy.

Sometimes we simply outgrow
what we used to know
that we couldn't live without.

And g r o w t h happens
when you decide to move along.

It is *so okay*
to k e e p it m o v i n g
in order to keep *choosing you.*

Choosing You

There is a fine -l-i-n-e-
between taking memories
out of s t o r a g e,
turning them in your hand
like a worry stone,
making them your

H

    O

       M

         E...

And knowing exactly
when to *leave them* a l o n e.

Memories

That moment
where the tide   t   s
              u   n
           r
is *everything*.

One moment...
      you are drowning in pain,

begging beaten lungs to work again;

you can all but h o l d yourself in.

And then?
when you least expect it,
you are b r e a t h i n g; on dry land

and it doesn't hurt as bad.

The Tide Turns

If ever one day
you sit and ruminate;
carefully contemplate
the agonizing choice...

"To stay or go to?"

I'd   rather   you   go.

I only need
the kind of

l

        o

              v

                  e

that *knows*
it belongs
in my tomorrows.

In My Tomorrows

Once upon a darkened time
in my ordinary life

              The world faded black.

              all was still and dark;

       Not even the stars
       could ignite the spark
       that would defibrillate
   and   r e a n i m a t e me.

I wished every puddle
were bottomless.

       I wished my heart,
       beating like a joke
       would know emptiness.

              I wished the sky
              above my head
              would cave in
                to nothingness.

I wished I were   d

                       e

                           a

                               d

      wiped from existence,
      from every memory
      I ever lived in.

      But that never happened...

And   in   time,
I started to slowly
wake again,
in fractions
of s m a l l actions,
I clawed the dirt
packed in above me
tentatively; then frenetically,
desperate to
F
R
E
E
me.

And then?
Light above me.
And before I knew it,
I was b r e a t h i n g.

It began
in quiet strength;

between breaths and sighs
and small moments.

And I have lived a little more
each day since.

Each Day Since

I am
a rose
in   f l u x.

My petals
once *dry as dust*
had
f
a
l
l
e
n.

And I spent so much time
watching them   *decay*   on the ground,
that I never bothered to look around me.

Once in flux;
now a bud,
who never saw- never knew
that she was back in   b l o o m.

Back in Bloom

Like *blunt-force trauma* to the head,
I was hit with the agonizing truth
that you will never
be able to realize my v a l u e.

Luckily?
Now I do.

People who don't even like me
treat me better than you do.

Which is why it's even more messed up,
that you used to worship us
and call it "love".

But now?
I've had
E
N
O
U
G
H.

Value

Take care to be careful
when you carefully starve her

          of appreciation and validation,
        like sunlight; until she suffocates.

      Because she will chase her way
        toward a new source
     of appreciation and affirmation,
   where   l   o   v   e   exists like oxygen.

      And in herself, she's planted
     in the *nourishment* she craves,
    bathed in the grace she needs.

She will then fully bloom
        in a space far away
            from the *grey* of you.

      And she will bear
  the s e e d s   o f   f o r t i t u d e,
    and then sow her *survival*
    fed down to her roots.

    And then straighten the crowns
    of other wilting flowers, too.

PhotosyntheSIS

I was looking for you
in all the places
our love *used to be...*

When,   a l l   a l o n g,
I should have been
looking for
m
e.

Lost and Bound

In

G

N

I

V

O

L

and then

L

O

S

I

N

G

you must end up *choosing yourself,*

over the hand
you've been dealt
by someone who is
deeply w o u n d e d themselves.

Self-Suture

For so long,

it had felt as though

I had dipped my pen

into my

o

w

n

b

l

o

o

d

to write of   y o u.

But now I know,

I don't need to *bleed*

for the truth...

The broken one

was always *you.*

The Broken One

Is it enough to b r e a t h e
when they question everything
you s t a n d for
and adore?

The ground
c
  a
   l
    l
     s
for my head,
though I'm standing on two feet.
They came for my c r o w n,
but it's not theirs for the taking.

There is no
b
 r
e
  a
k
i
  n
g
me.

STOP trying.

Unbroken

"I'm sorry"
will   a l w a y s

taste

like

a c i d

when uttered for

c

r

i

m

e

s

that you didn't commit.

We were never taught
to
acquit
ourselves;
but it's time we   d i d.

Misplaced Apologies

Silence is a golden sound
        when you're trying to
                get to know yourself.

        Be still;
        listen
        to the voice within.

        Let your heartbeat
        charge your skin
with electric   c u r r e n t...

        humming
                a new frequency;

        tuning you back
        into *y o u.*

A New Frequency

I used to wait for closure.

I used to crave it.

I used to think I needed it...

In order to move on.

In order to forgive.

In order *to feel right* again.

It took a long time to learn

that closure comes from within;

Not from *anyone else,*

but from the soul of the s e l f.

Closure

It's strange
how we can gain
the l o v e we've wanted,
but convince ourselves
We don't deserve it.

We can achieve *success*,
And then think
We didn't earn it...
Even if we worked tirelessly
To attain it.

How is it
that we believe
so steadfastly
in the dark
t h a t binds u s,

but push away the
l
i
g
h
t
whenever it finds us?

Paradox

If you were thinking

    of coming back around;

          Stay.
          The.
          Hell.
          Away.

    I am learning
to   l o v e myself,

    and you'd just
    get in the way.

Stay Away

If love wasn't blind,
as far the eye could see,
there'd be no reasoning
with the mind always   r u n n i n g   away with me.

If love wasn't blind,
I would *choose a little kindness.*
I'd cover my heart in roses,
and tell it to   h o l d   s t e a d y.

If love wasn't blind,
I might already be ready
to *shed the pain* like a second skin;
to wipe my face and   r i s e   again.

If love wasn't blind,
I wouldn't need reminding
to cocoon myself with   g r a c e,
and learn *the subtle art of patience.*

If love wasn't blind,
I'd *hold myself* in the night,
quiet and calm; forever within sight
of the sun inside me;   r i s i n g.

If love wasn't blind,
I'd *come home* like the   t i d e,
lapping at the   s a f e t y   of shore,
tired of the weightless sky.

If love wasn't blind,
I'd memorize my reflection
from the *gentler perspective*
of all those who   l o v e   and   v a l u e   me.

If love wasn't blind,
I'd *unleash my light* unto the world,
hold a magnifying glass to it;
watch it   u n d u l a t e   and unfurl.

But love **isn't** blind;
it just wears   b l i n d e r s   sometimes,
and they can, in time, *be removed.*
One day, you will finally see (clearly),

that you were only   b l i n d   to loving ***you***...

and you have *a lot of catching up to do*.

If Love Wasn't Blind

I am a glorious mess.
I am the chaos of stars.
I am a disaster in m
o
t
i
o
n.

My devotion to using up
every ounce of my essence
creates my trails of dust.

My
f
r
e
n
z
i
e
d
energy
precedes every room I walk into;
last to enter is my body.

My eyes speak in t o n g u e s...
a second language birthed
by the fire of the

s

u

n.

Hear me.
Fear me.
See me.

I am a l i v i n g storm.
I am coming.

This world cannot

c   n

  o   i

   n   a

    t

me.

Essence

The more time I spend
in d e e p introspection,
the more I *despise the sight*
of my own reflection.

The *cruelty* that I show myself
is a far cry
from the compassion
that I show everyone else.

And I don't know how to fix it
because as easily as I b r e a t h e,
I pick myself

a

p

a

r

t;

completely.

It turns out,
that my *own worst enemy*
l i v e s m o r e close t o h o m e
than I'd ever known.

But not for long...

Mirror, Mirror

You are worth FAR more
than the voice inside your head
that *lies*...

You are NOT worthless.
You are NOT alone.
You are NOT better off gone.

You ARE loved.
You ARE valued.

And just because, for now
you've lost "you"
doesn't make it
ANY less true.

Chains and pain won't keep you down forever,
and I will be here to watch you *get better.*

I Will Be Here

My skin has always been so pliable,
and by now
it must damn near have healing powers.

As many times as stars in the sky,
I have   c u t   it open
and beat hate into my own blood....

N

O...

N

O !

NOT. GOOD. ENOUGH.

The vessel supposed to be my home,
is the prison where I die alone;
an unconscious decision to view with derision
what I only know how to despise...

I wondered if the disease leaves in my eyes.

So, I burned them   *blind.*
And then proceeded to pour bleach in my brain,
send poison through my veins,
lobotomize the pain away.

All. The. World's. A. Stage....

And at the end of the scene,
I stand;
in defeated finality,

D

   R

      I

         P

            P

               I

                  N

                     G,

dripping...

Torn shards of doubt splatter,
with the shatters of a soul
that feels *so much older*
than the constellations sewn into my skin;
scars like stars from the needle and thread
that I have to walk around with
for the next time I f l a y myself open again.

Why

     Why

         Why

              do I do this...

A rag doll;

an object of "no".

pock marks from acid infiltrating her bones.

Their marrow

l

e

a

k

s

out

and sows

Reaped seeds of self-loathing

that

GROW

AND GROW

AND GROW...

This sad, bloody thing

in crudely-stitched skin,

stands in a field of bloom,

rotting in a meadowed tomb.

The world outside *adores her,*
but the mind inside   a b h o r s   her.
Thus the gifted crown of flowers
hits her head and

w

i

t

h

e

r

s

So she writes love into   t h o r n s,
and ignores the rose.

And so

it *goes...*

Heavy is the Head

It is all too easy to be our own worst enemy, isn't it?

My heart was once a h o a r d e r' s house;
I *lived*
and *breathed*
and tiptoed around
my own b a g g a g e.

It was always
covering the floors,
preventing me from
moving
freely...
Through life;
through rooms
I n e v e r cleaned.

But I found
that when I started taking care of me...
it all began disappearing.

Now?
My floors are
clear
and
clean.

Baggage Claim

I SEE YOU:
The "you" that you hide from the world.

I see the miniscule   c r a c k s
in the façade of the smile
you painted on,
after   p l e a d i n g   with the dawn
to be a little kinder
than the night had been.

Forget   new   beginnings.

I see that you can't believe
in the certainty
of anything but endings.

And I see you watching nothing but
S
  U
    N
      S
        E
          T
            S

because sunrises are promises
the sun *never kept*...
and you now never rely on constants,
because they **feel** like the truth....
but then they go and pull the rug out from under you.

Apparently they had a "plan"
that you will n e v e r understand.

You feel so far removed
from the reality you didn't choose.
Every step; every breath-a precipice,
one small misstep
and you're free-falling...

but not even your dreams will catch you.

Each day, you wake,
and you fake it til you make it,
and you steel yourself to survive the day.
"Never let them see you break"...

But break, you do.
Every day, in a million ways
because grief
and loss
and broken hearts
Stay. And stay. *And stay.*

No, they don't see you. But I do.
I see you.
Because **I am you.**

I See You

I am something
forged by flames,
and scarred by

P

    A

      I

        N...

No, I will never be the same,
but I like this version of me better anyway.
Change...
    hard   e d g e s   gone,
molded into something soft.

And when I find myself lost,
finding the light again will cost
nothing more than what I've learned.

First, I had to burn
before I could learn
the wisdom that taught me
g r e a t e r   love,
and e m p a t h y
that lives within...

and never leaves...

Change

81

Of all the things

I have come to know,

like the back of my hand,
like the comfort of home,
or the marrow of my bones;

I know this...

time is both fleeting and infinite.

It renews and it makes.

It creates and it breaks.

But more than anything?

Eventually; it takes.

It makes oceans of tears

and   m i n u t e s   of years.

In its indifferent hands,

nothing transient stands a chance...

Second chances.

Last meals.

First dances.

Lost romances.

Words never said...

time controls   a   l   l   of them...

You. Me. And everything.

I arrived with a wrinkle,
and I'll depart with a   r i p p l e,
in the grand scheme and tapestry
that weaves me firmly into the world.

One day, I will go quiet-
but not in the way you think.

Someday there will be nobody left
who remembers my name.

But the depth with which I loved
while I shared space here,
will be both everything...
and   *n o t h i n g.*

So, while I'm here, my cross to bear
is just to live;
to use myself up
until I am dust
that I hope floats back up into the stars.

And maybe you'll be somewhere not too far.
and maybe the memory of my heart
will echo,
until it remembers yours...

Echo

If you strip away the love
and the lies
and the mess
and the distress you caused
giving me nothing at all...
I am left with nothing *but "Nothings"*.

"Nothings" that I wish had been "Somethings".

I never asked for "Everythings".

But I deserved more
than a broken heart
and false starts
and pretty words that hit their mark,
like venom; like poison.

Through my unsuspecting lips,
you tainted what was sacred.

And it turns out
that even bottomless wells
can be tapped dry
with "Maybes" and silences and lies;
that you left me
to clean up
(alone) this time.

Now...
a round of applause
for tirelessly inventing
new ways
to disappoint me
with nothing
but "Nothings".

So,
I gathered all your "Nothings"
and I turned them into "Everythings"
that I will save

for someone
more deserving.

Nothings

Please.

Don't.

Go.

I know...
I'm buried in sediment.

But
the best of me
is under here yet.

I.

Promise.

It.

Sediment

Love me   c o m p l e t e l y

and wildly
and unconditionally
                        for all the pieces of me
        you may not always love.

        You might not always
                            U
                    N
                            D
                                E
                                    R
                                S
                            T
                        A
                    N
                D

        but if you *take my hand*
            and <u>never let go,</u>
        your love will guide me home
            when I lose myself
        and forget where I belong...

When I Lose Myself

Self-loathing is inaccuracy -
a sapling
that becomes a tree;

        watered with inadequacy.

And then shading you
from the t r u t h....

overtaking
the best of you.

The Tree

LET NOTHING DIM THE LIGHT
THAT SHINES FROM WITHIN.

MAYA ANGELOU

How many times
have you melted into the floor in your mind?

How many times
have you gazed at cracks in the earth...

praying that they would   s w a l l o w   you whole?

How many times
have   you   tried   to   shrink   yourself   invisible?

There is a reason that you can't, you know.

You are meant:
To glow.
To grow.
To hope.
To reach for more.

Meant for More

You cannot hitch a free ride
on the wings of my heart anymore.

They are forged by   f i r e   and velvet
and you are now the discarded paper
you once treated my love as.

The flames are catching,
and the rain is coming.

You will not survive.

B
  U
    T

   I

WILL.

Fire & Rain

A n x i e t y
is living with an apple on your head,

and you imagine
that   e   v   e   r   y   o   n   e   you know,
stands watching with a

b

o

w,

to *shoot* an arrow at it...

and

m
i
s
s
.

Anxiety

It is quiet*; silent*
in the   spaces   between me
where nothing   b r e a t h e s,
nothing moves,
and nobody leaves.

There is stillness
to   fill   the   gaps
of my lapses in memory,
spanning the *darker days*
where my forest spent burning.

The fire is unlearning
the former heart of me.
Now s t r o n g e r; playing for keeps,
I'm replaced the pain with a box of change
that Time placed in my hands....

I used to want to
G
      I
            V
                  E
                        it back...
but I've learned it never works like that.

In it are moments; figments
now   *carefully*   kept at bay,
though I don't want
to keep them safe...
(please   carry   them   away).

Fairweather   f l i c k e r s,
swirling like *triggers,*
awaiting my finger having an off-day;
to   -p-r-e-s-s-   like a bruise,
old blood in the wound,

to prove I can   hold   them-
and still feel

o

k

a

y...

Fairweather Flickers

Getting to know *myself* again

was

as

easy

(and as difficult)

as   p i c k i n g   up

a   pen....

Picking Up A Pen

Dear today,

please

go   e a s y   on me.

I spent the night awake; *half-alive*

being the usual amount of "unkind" to myself.

Dear sun,

please

s h i n e   on me.

My heart has been so *heavy,*

and I need some peace.

Dear self,

please

learn to   l o v e   *you,*

the way everyone else seems to.

Dear

You came into my heart;

finger-painted our

love

into

life.

and though you might have   l e f t ...

The colors never did.

I hold them sacred;

deep

within.

You wouldn't stay,

but I'm keeping them.

Sacred

When I stopped *blaming myself*

for

e

v

e

r

y

little thing

that was wrong

in and   *a*   *d*

r   *n*

o *u*

my life...

I shed the "wrongs",

and found the "right".

The Right

I learned the hard way

that time doesn't   w a i t.

And so, I choose

to *speak the truth*...

Even if it comes out in waves.

Even if I   c h o k e.

Even if I   s t u t t e r.

Even if my *tongue gets tied*.

I am only here but once,

and I do not *trust* in time.

I Choose Truth

Through the thin veil of d r e a m s,
I visit an earlier version of me.
I greet her like an old friend;
Outstretched hand and e m p a t h y.

"Oh, my darling..."

Not a few years later,
Life will steal her symmetry.
She will d i e unto all she knew...
And re-emerge as me.

As the veil later blurs,
And she begins to slip away,
I warmly wish her well,
And promise I am here to s t a y.

She will find me someday,
At the end of her rope...
Inside of herself;
Hope b l o o m i n g her home.

I will w a i t for her.

I Will Wait

I have found
That the
      lasting
        love
          I seek

comes to me
quietly; unexpectedly,
when I'm *not*   l o o k i n g.

And usually,
it comes
      from
        me.

Lasting Love

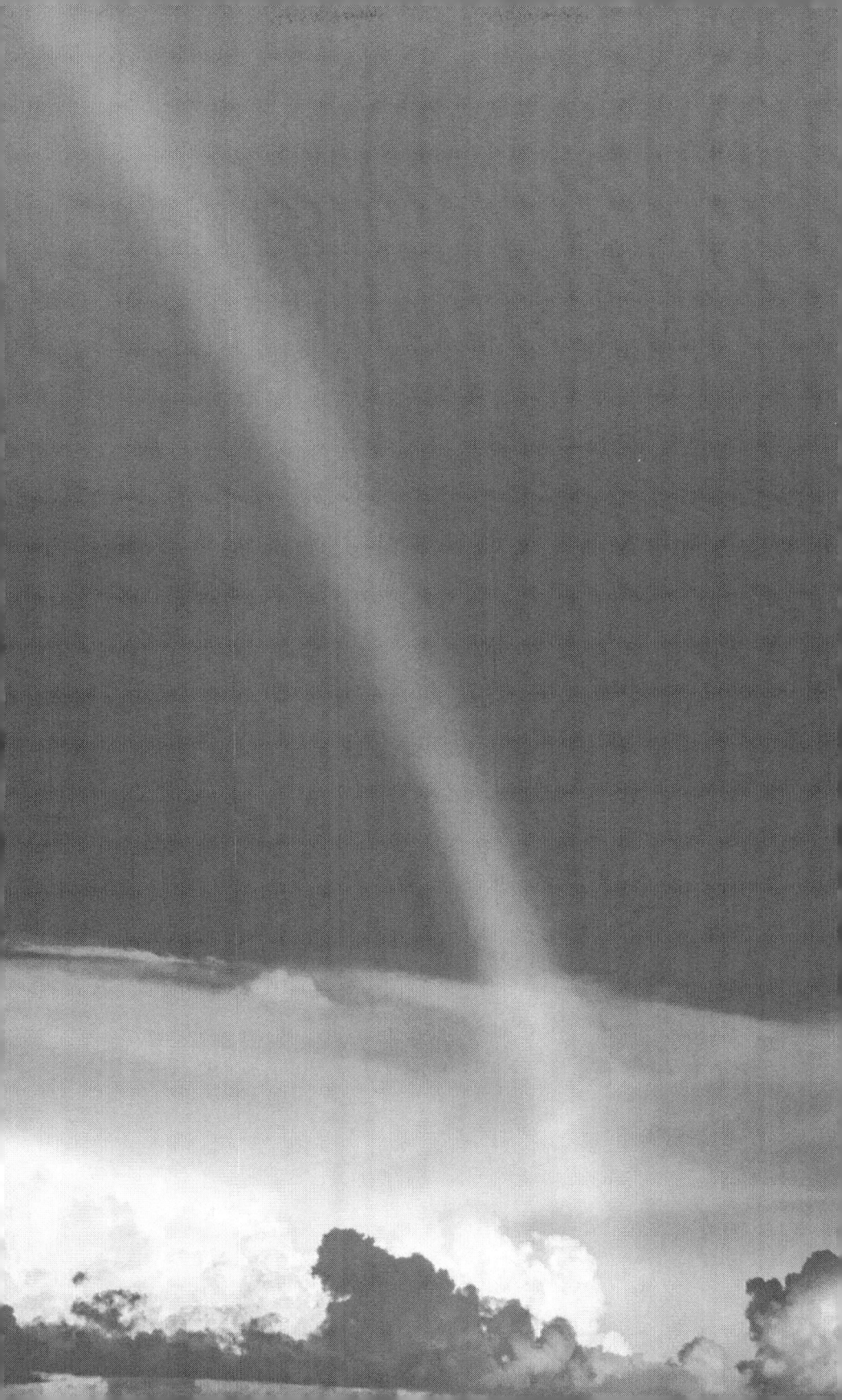

When our eyes first met,
I knew I was staring at
My   r u i n.
My   u n d o i n g.
My greatest   r e g r e t.

And yet
I
still
ignored
the warnings in my mind-
telling me to *run away,*
before it's   too   late.

Now I'm here...
bleeding; fumbling blindly
gathering
the
pieces
of my heart and life
that you *tore away* from me.

There is a lesson here...

when you see a walking   b u l l s e y e,
you don't fancy yourself an   a r r o w...

you

     turn

        and

            run

        and

         continue,

until there's nothing left behind you.

One sweet day,
when I'm in one piece again,
I will have the   w   i   s   d   o   m
to the honor the
sanctity

    of

       my

        own

          heart

from the *start.*

My love is a   g   i   f   t,
and you should have *honored* it.

Lesson Learned, Wisdom Earned

When you don't know   w h e r e   to go,

or which   r o a d   to follow,

choose the direction

of your own   a

                      r

                              r

                                      o

                                            w.

It will always
lead you   h o m e.

Your Arrow

Poetry?

That's easy.

I just   c u t   the vein,
and let it
b

l

e

e

d.

The paper *absorbs my story*
indiscriminately;
the   b e a u t y,   the   u g l y
the *journey*...

and   e v e r y t h i n g
In between.

Poetry

Have the

A

U

D

A

C

I

T

Y

to be   *a f r a i d.*

And then?

Do it

A

N

Y

W

A

Y

.

The Audacity

My wayard ship

S

A

N

K

but I *escaped;*
and swam up
to the   s u r f a c e   again.

I have since learned
to live
and love
with "wreck"less abandon.

Wreckless

Somewhere *deep within* a drawer,
lives a l e t t e r   I wrote to you...
a *pillar* to the stars
I once thought of you.

I imagine you have
burnt it,
and long *forgotten*
the ashes.

But I haven't.

And I find
that after   a l l   t h i s   t i m e,
I no longer need
your apology.

I know it's <u>never</u> coming,
and it no longer matters...
I've got <u>me</u>.

I've Got Me

I love the quiet;

the stillness of the night...

the   M u s e s   find me then.

It's almost as if

the   d y i n g   of the light outside,

makes it come to life
within.

Quiet of the Night

I do not need
you to be *welcoming*.

Should you choose
not to *include me,*

I can bring my own seat,
to my own table,
that I am able
to create;
to *hold space for myself.*

Table for One

I hope
that the fervor
of my passion in this life

burns further on,
long after I am   g o n e.

I want to go
in a grand crescendo:

where every   o u n c e   of love
I ever bestowed
echoes
on,
around,
and then
D
O
W
N...
back into the world.

Grand Crescendo

Thank you for *leaving*
and *lying* to me.
you gave me endless   p o e t r y.

If you had stayed,
and the pen had stilled,
where on earth would I be now?

You *stole my heart,*
but I *kept the words.*
And I will keep

spilling

them

out...

one by one.

Until every last piece of you
is

G
O
N
E.

I Kept The Words

Tonight, the skies are   c l e a r i n g.
The fire dances   f l a m e s into my eyes.
The earth   *hums*   beneath my feet.
The wind sings   h y m n s   to the trees.
The moon stands guard; listening.

I am finally ready;

m

o

l

t

i

n

g.

The second-skin prison
has   l o o s e n e d   just enough
for me to begin
peeling
it
off.

And tonight?
I want to throw it on the   f l a m e s
and   *breathe*   my own name
into the rest of my   l i f e.

The Art of Rising

I hope the dawn   b r e a k s
in a tidal wave of butterflies;
washing away your unrelenting pain.

For when the moon rises,
like *bile* in your throat,
you beg away the darkness
and slowly   l o s e   *yourself.*

I have been there, too.
And I hope that, someday,
you believe in   f l i g h t   again.

Until then...
I will wait,
and keep you   s a f e.

I can hold the monsters at bay
until the day you see
that every   s i n i s t e r   shadow
swaying outside your window...

is nothing but *a*   t r e e.

Until the Day

After you,
I was a stranger.

There was not a single cell within me that you had not altered.
Everything I knew about myself and my life became foreign.

I erected altars to what became the death of me.
I thought false gods of the "you" in my memory.

Mirrors became enemies;
magnets for shame.

I would stare for days,
and not even know who I was looking at...or even for.

My eyes had hardened.
They were duller, colder, and grayer than I remembered.
You emptied storms into them.

I accepted your rain and sent it back out to you through my eyes.
I withered like the roses you gave that I left in the vase to die.
I killed them like you killed the world's simplest equation:
$1+1=2$.

I once thought that "home" was a place you had taken with you...

It wasn't.

"Home" lives within the very skin you haven't touched in months.
It's in the eyes that have since returned to vibrancy.
It's here in the life and routine and body of the woman you're
missing;
the one you regret letting go.

But she's not where you left her anymore.

She's *home*.

Rainbow

You

are

never

too

far

gone....

You Can Always Come Home

(Prose)

Spent, unwanted love can feel like it's killing you.

But it doesn't have to.

Take it; gather it up.

Then? Instead of aiming it at someone who doesn't want or value it, unleash it out into the world around you.

Love has the ability to multiply itself when it is well-received. Stop wasting the best of you on the worst of your past.

Love Multiplies

If something or someone must be so carefully kept or so gingerly tended, then it is likely not for you.

What is meant for you will not be so fragile and uncertain.

You will be able to test it; to flex its capabilities. You will not be so afraid that a breeze blown through fearful lips will be enough to knock it down.

Not Yours

It hurts, but you must remember...

not everyone has your heart.

Not everyone loves like you do.

Just as your own brand of love is rare,

rare is the person who can match it.

Rare Heart

If I ever loved you, if you ever meant something to me...

You will always be a part of me.

We will always share a connection.

A tether; a link remains.

Always.

A Link Remains

"Survival", in reality, little resembles the way it's usually portrayed.

It doesn't always scream and shake its fists.

It is often quiet.

It is, at times, a small ghost of a whisper that tells you that tomorrow, you will try again...

To wake.

To stand.

To put one foot in front of the other.

To force a smile.

To just *try*.

Quiet Survival

Some days, it is nearly impossible to be kind to yourself.

It is nearly impossible to get out of bed;

to face a day you're not ready for.

The voices in your head will scream that you're not good enough.

Your anxieties will become living, breathing things.

It is okay to take time.

It is okay to retreat back into yourself.

It's okay to move slowly, or not move at all.

It's okay to hide when your mind needs silence.

It's okay to not be okay.

And it's okay to give yourself grace.

Some Days

A feather in the wind;

you'll drift.

You will come to rest

far from where you began...

and land where you are meant to.

Feather

Healing is much like gardening.

You begin to clear away the old, dead things. You pull weeds, remove debris, and turn the soil.

I like to think that it **knows**. The earth, so alive in its own right, can *FEEL* that love and care is about to poured back into it.

It wakes up.

Humans are just like that. With empathetic touch, pain eventually subsides and we can finally breathe around the hurt that stole our lungs. We give ourselves over intuitively to the care that is given to us.

We, at our very core, crave our own restoration...

And so, into the dug-out earth go seeds and saplings. We water their root systems, mulch the beds surrounding them, and blanket them securely in the earth.

We give the time, patience, and space to g r o w.

And those tiny, little seeds? Those weak, tender shoots?

They grow. They thrive. They bloom.

And so will you.

The Healing Garden

As tempting as it is, never wish you could go back and do a piece of your life over.

If even one single detail were changed, you could be leading

a completely different life.

Trust that despite the struggles and storms you have weathered, you are *right where you should be.*

Trust your path;

Always.

The Path

There is a porch-light deep inside each of us.

At certain points, that light disappears. Either the wiring gets faulty or the bulb burns out. Regardless, the reason it is broken does not matter, because the resulting darkness is the same.

That porch light is our gateway to home. Not "home" as in four walls, windows, and rooms...

"Home" as in the core of who we are.

"Home" as in the matter of which we are made.

"Home" as in the housing of our souls.

This light contains the essence of you.

What a beautiful truth it is to learn that no matter how long that light has been out, it *can* be turned back on. It *can* shine again. It can be fixed.

And so can **you.**

Porch Light

When you suffocate under the weight of your own self-doubt,

Go outside at night.

Look up.

You are a piece of all that you see.

There is "divine" within you.

Just like the magnetic pull of the stars,

And the majesty of the moon;

There are mysteries and magic in you.

There is a reason we are drawn to the sky.

It is because we know that deep within us,

There is stardust.

We are a piece of the universe.

Small though we may be,

There is something old and mighty in our souls.

So, let your axis tilt.

You will find your symmetry again.

Let Your Axis Tilt

You may find that you need to light yourself on fire
to burn the "broken" away.

Whatever you do?
Never apologize for the ashes.

Phoenix

You may think that being moved to *move* means you are discontent with what you have. That is simply not true.

This is just your soul craving adventure. To see what you have not seen. To explore what remains wild and elusive.

There are always answers to be found.

They tend to hide in plain sight.

There is an explorer inside all of us. Heed the call.

Wanderlust

Go.

I feel your restlessness.

I see your darting eyes.

I take in your shaking hands.

You long to fly;

Away from what you know.

You want to find a new piece of this earth

To call your own;

To scatter your soul like stardust.

So go.

Go elsewhere in this big, wide world.

Find your place in it.

You want to run your fingers

Through unfamiliar earth.

Discover. Learn. Heal yourself.

You can always come home.

You Can Always Come Home

Always remember that you are *NEVER* required to keep anyone around who is detrimental to your own mental health and healing.

Protect your own heart and mind first. Relentlessly. At all costs.

It is the *ONLY* way to be any good to anyone else.

Read.

That.

Again.

First? You.

One of the hardest lessons in life is learning when to dig in your heels and hang on for dear life, and when to take a deep breath and

l

e

t

g

o.

At some point, you have to just trust that souls know their way home.

What is meant for you will find you. *And stay.*

Letting Go

We are all wounded.

Every single one of us is riddled with unseen holes and covered with invisible-ink scars.

However, being wounded is *never* an excuse or a valid reason to wound someone else.

You cannot heal by inflicting pain.

Wounded

When we

L

     E

       T

                  G

                     O...

We set

o u r s e l v e s

f

r

e

e.

Set Free

I don't think it is any accident that the strongest people are the ones who have been through the most.

They are battle-tested. Their skin is thick. They are scarred.

They intimately know pain and how to stand up again. They are soldiers of battles unknown. They are consummate survivors.

But their most special sort of magic?

Despite what they have endured, their hearts so often remain warm and empathetic. That is nothing short of a miracle.

Amethyst Heart

I used to think that "alone" meant "lonely".

Now? I live for the pleasure of my own company.

My Own Company

Let your struggles harden you like a diamond in the rough.

Know that you are   e   n   o   u   g   h

exactly *where* you are,

and just *as you are*.

Every cut that you have withstood

is now one of your facets.

Let them hone you until you sparkle,

scintillating through the rainbows

you have waited so long to find.

(You just never knew

That they lived *within* you).

Diamond Mine

One of the most humanizing revelations we can have is to realize that we have put our happiness in the hands of others for too long.

Often? For *all our lives*.

Luckily, we can turn it around.

Start treating yourself with the dignity and compassion that you bestow upon others.

It is just that simple. It is just that hard.

Turn It Around

Stop losing sleep over someone who *doesn't even dream* about you.

Sleep Soundly

Look at everything you have been through.

And you are *still* here. You are still standing.

You are a warrior. You are not the "easy kill".

You were b o r n to survive.

Still Here

There is always *that one person* to whom we owe a debt.

We once thought they would be our own undoing. They broke our heart, did us wrong, or refused to believe in us.

But, in the end, they show us who we are, what we are capable of, and what we deserve.

We can thank them for teaching us to know better, and then thank ourselves for turning pain into wisdom.

Thank You

The best revenge is ALWAYS the glow-up.

Want to get even?

Get up, show up, and *show out*.

Rise. Shine. Glow. Be impossible to ignore.

Glow-Up

Behind your trust issues and excess caution, there is an unspoken apology. There is an "I'm sorry" that never came.

In time, you will heal just fine without it.

Unsaid Apology

You may have once thought you were writing the greatest romance this world has ever seen.

What seems like a heartbeat later, you are crumpled in a heap on the ground; cutting yourself on your own broken pieces.

But your story? No, it's not a tragedy.

It's a comeback in the making.

You will not stay this broken, defeated creature forever.

I promise.

Comeback

Someday, somewhere down the line...

You will be able to think of *that* person without going to pieces.
Tears will no longer sting your eyes.

The memories will no longer have serrated edges.

The pain you feel now? You won't live in that anymore. Heartbreak
is no longer your home. Your new home is *you*.

Someday, it is all going to change.

Time will make you wistfully grateful

For what that person taught you.

Nothing more.

Nothing less.

Nothing More, Nothing Less

Time steals, but it also heals.

So allow yourself to feel what you feel.

Sit in your "broken" long enough for it to start looking like "hope" again. Eventually, it will.

In Time

Loss is a seed that implants within.

Every fallen tear waters it.

And in time, it grows higher and higher. It climbs.

A timeless contradiction.

A weight you are able to carry in time.

A tree that you learn to live around.

Grief

I would hang my life upon your lips; the perfect weapon.

I would make your heart my final resting place.

Hold me tight; I'm coming home.

The Perfect Weapon

We speak of our hearts like they are things to give away.

They are not.

They are ours alone, and only meant to be shared with care.

Our Hearts

We are all merely the sum of all of our formative voices.

Some of us were fortunate to have been built-up.

Some of us were torn down before we even had a chance to rise.

In adulthood, we hold the power to control what we listen to and what we tune out. Let your own voice always scream the loudest.

Voices

Do not let your pain

Steal away the things that bring you joy.

Let your joys be your tourniquet.

Let them stitch your wounds.

You need them most when you are lost.

What Brings You Joy

Traumas may be a part of you.

But they do not have to **become** you.

(There is a difference between the two).

You are so much more than the sum of your scars.

So Much More

I am not "too much". I never was.

The truth is, you were not "enough" to hold me.

I am a flame; a storm. I burn my way through this life with a passion that consumes me and everything in my path. One day, I will rage my way out of this world. Even then, I will not go quietly.

I am brave and fearless when you are scared and cautious. I am direct and open when your tongue gets tied. You stare at your hands when I try to meet your eyes.

What else was there for us in the end but "Goodbye"?

I was "too much" for you, because, deep down, you knew that you never deserved me.

Too Much

Give yourself the courtesy of imperfection.

At the end of the day, you are only human.

You will succeed. You will struggle. You will fly. You will fall.

It is all a part of the experience. And it all matters.

Only Human

I am now only at home in the light because I know darkness all too well.

You must walk through fire before you can appreciate the cooling sensation of healing.

Well-Versed

When it's all you can do not to collapse under the weight of all the baggage you're carrying, you must remember to breathe.

There are times you will have to focus on nothing but the air entering and leaving your lungs...or you will come completely undone.

Breathe

When I was a child,

I used to fear monsters under the bed.

I have since learned that most monsters are found within.

And they are always worth fighting.

Monsters

Life has this way of taking all the wind out of our sails.

Even so; we are never directionless.

We may not be able to control the winds, but we often forget our anchors. Everyone who loves us is there, beneath the surface, rooting us into ourselves when we feel we are about to scatter into the wind.

Let go. And lean into it.

Anchors

When you are lost, just remember...

You will not stay lost forever.

Learn to make peace with mystery.

Learn to trust the ground underneath your feet.

Learn to give yourself over to gravity.

Sooner or later,

You will know which path to follow.

You Will Not Stay Lost

Self love?

I am no guru. I am no oracle. I am no expert.

I have no magic advice that will teach you how to love yourself. I have clichés. I have the usual wisdom that sounds pretty and gets repeated often.

For me? The reality is that I am still learning. I am still healing. I am still trying to put trauma and grief in my rearview mirror. I fail every single day at this concept called "self love".

Regardless, I still try. I get up the next day and try to heal just a little more; hold on just a little longer; try just a little harder.

I have a sneaking suspicion that this IS the journey; the key to what I seek. It's in trying, failing, and then trying again.

It's in not giving in. And appreciating yourself for it.

Self Love

I am just a rose; hoping someone will notice my thorns and *pick me anyway*... knowing that I am worth it.

The Rose

It took me so long to understand that what broke us was your own, deep brokenness.

I wanted to fix what was never mine to fix in the first place.

I lost so much of myself disappearing into you.

I will never make that mistake again.

I hope every day for your wounds to heal. I hold the best of us in my heart, and I still believe that the best is yet to come for you.

Brokenness

One of my hardest lessons was learning to be content in stillness.

I do not need to engage with what I cannot win.

I do not need to withstand what will not bring me peace.

I can choose to breathe in the space of stillness,

and let the storms pass overhead.

Stillness

Stand at my door;

knock endlessly.

I can and will not allow you back in.

I have to choose what is good for me.

We both know *you never will be*.

Knock

In the arrival of your hurricane, you painted my world grey.

The color leaked out of every crack and corner of this life I used to know.

Right now, the eye of your storm is passing overhead. I am enjoying being able to catch my breath.

I know what is coming next. And I am ready.

Hurricane

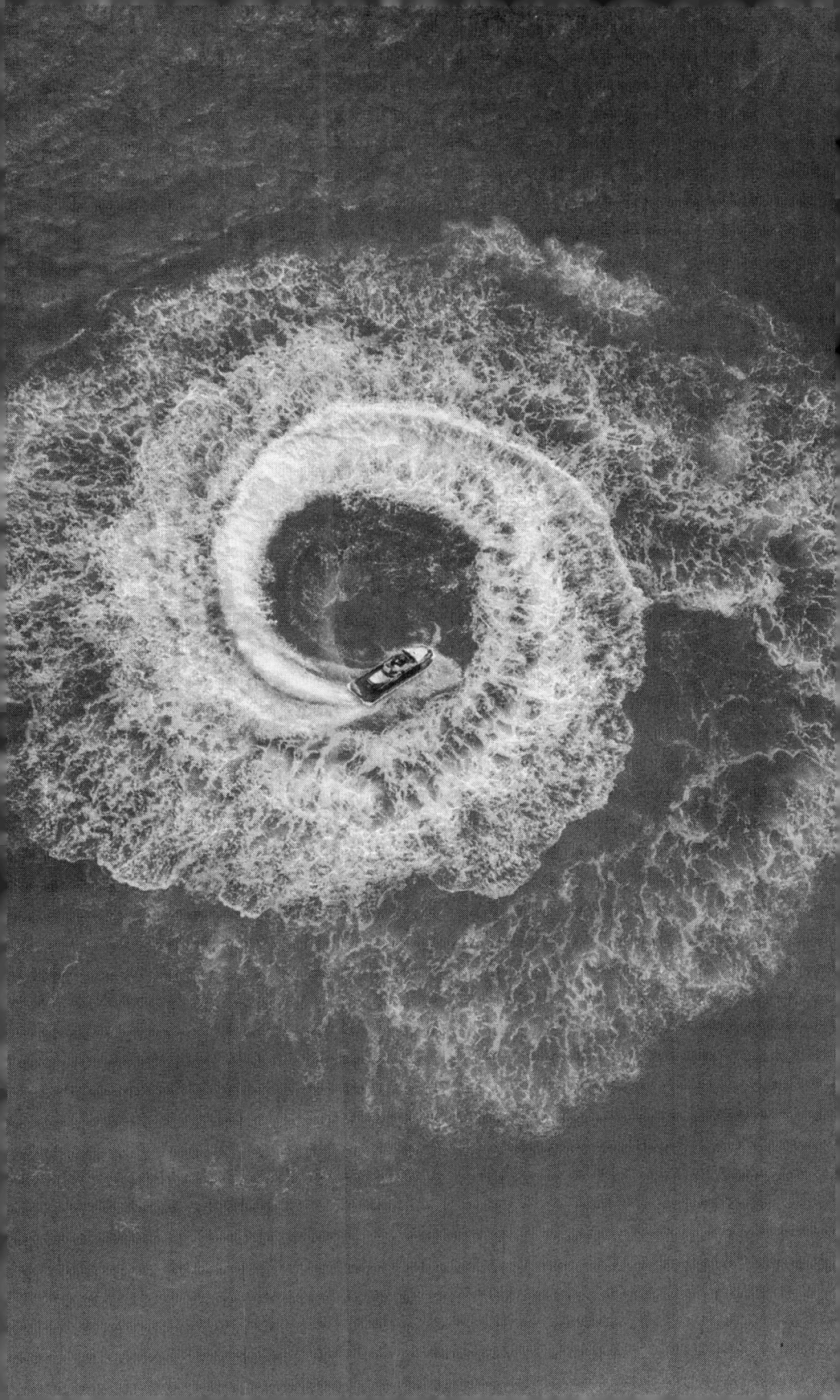

ph Homecoming | Stefanie Briar

I fall headlong into everything that lights me on fire.

I know not of restraint.

I was

      born

           to

                b u r n.

Born to Burn

To those barely breathing;

Hang on.

Every wound, every loss, and every lie is attached to you like your spinal cord. They control your every thought, your every emotion, and even your every movement.

They wield enough power to convince you that you are dying even as you take a deep breath.

One day, they will quiet. Their shouting will fade into a steady hum, and eventually taper off into a whisper.

Then? Silence...

Beautiful, welcomed, blissful silence.

One Day, They Will Go Quiet

I used to want you to miss me.

It used to be a desire as visceral as the need to be near you; to inhale you; to take you back home into the heart of me.

I no longer spend time hoping that the memory of me annihilates you. I hope the opposite is true.

I hope you learned something. I hope you inflict less harm in the future. I hope you grow. I wish you wisdom.

I hope you catch my scent in the wind, hear my voice in a song, see my eyes in the sea...and smile wistfully.

Let the bitterness fade, and the beauty remain.

I Used To

There is no other magic in life quite like blowing the dust off your own heart.

There are times where we place our own hearts up on lonely shelves; a self-imposed exile.

One day, when we are ready, we decide to use it again. What was once dusty, forgotten, and dormant now teems with life and possibility. And possibility means believing in "maybe".

Blowing Off Dust

What was the moment that told me I was getting better?

The end of the "wind tunnel".

For so long; SO long,

Life spun around me with its omnipresent hum.

I heard a constant, buzzing rhythm above the din of silence, but I could never pull any of it into focus.

I heard life carry on around me in wind-tunnel echo; an uncomfortable vacuum of white noise.

I woke up one day, and was surprised to hear clearly. The world was no longer miles away. I was *present*. That was the moment I knew that healing was not going to elude me forever.

The Moment I Knew

I once thought dried flowers were heartbreaking; pale, crumbling, withered vestiges of their former glory.

I have grown to love them.

They are memory-markers; reminders. They say "I was once vibrant and alive. Now, my beauty has faded, but my significance remains". What once was loved; stays.

Dried Flowers

Your body is no temple.

Your heart is an abandoned house.

All is dark and cold.

I am coming in, and I am bringing my warmth with me. I will turn on the lights in every single little corner of your soul. I will hold you until you feel whole again...

If only for a moment.

I Am Coming In

Even in the midst of turbulence; of storms-

When all is rocky, chaotic, and dim...

There is a calm center hidden within us all.

Sometimes it shines like a stadium light,

And sometimes it's about as strong as a candle in the rain.

Either way, it's there. The moment when you find it again is everything.

Calm Center

I have always been one for grand gestures. I'm awestruck by the abandon, gumption, and fearlessness that they require.

The few I've done in my life have been loud. You could see them; hear them coming. They typically carry all the subtlety of freight trains and neon signs.

That's why it stole my breath to quietly realize that my greatest grand gesture; my last, best act of love...

was to let you go.

Grand Gesture

"What makes you happy?"

The people I love. Sunbathing. The smell after it rains. A hug that knits you back into one piece for a while. Writing. The ocean. Roses. A cold drink on a hot day. Cake. A good book. Music.

Only one of those is a big thing. The rest are little things. I've always preferred the small things and their tiny details. The big picture tends to hurt, and focusing on that widens the chasm within me. Between the divide, there is a creeping numbness; a vast void that is effortless to fall into. I don't know how to explain, except to say that the little things help create a bridge. They line up and then fuse themselves together so I can cross over to another day.

I get really tired. And sometimes, I can't bring the little things into view enough to want to continue.

Most people have "off" days or bad days; they're normal. But mental illness is different and omnipresent. With mental illness, you have good days...

Because inner turmoil and pain _are_ your baseline.

It Feels Like This

If you struggle, know that you are NEVER alone!

Life is a journey...

We all hope that life will be long.

Whether or not mine is, I hope my words will leave an echo.

These words are all I have to give.

They are my legacy.

I'm still learning...to heal; to hold my own power; to let go; to breathe around loss and trauma and brokenness.

Learning to make peace with who I am and show myself love is my greatest goal in this life.

Hold me to it.

And as for you, my beautiful readers...

I wish you healing.

I wish you love.

I wish you light that holds you and won't let you go.

If you are lost,

I wish you a profound journey back to yourself,

Full of lessons learned along the way.

The beautiful truth is that the lost typically never stay lost forever.

Light has a way of fighting its way back in.

Always look for it.

Love,

S.B.

Happy Homecoming.

The Words Are Your Own

(Journal)

The following pages are here for you if you would like to use them. There are no lines because there are no rules.

Consider this to be journal space for writing your own words.

Think, feel, breathe, and create something.

Epilogue

In truth, I thought long and hard about how I wanted to "leave" this book. How could I ever begin to sum up the transformative, cathartic, beautiful experience of putting <u>Homecoming</u> together?

The answer came to me unexpectedly, as many answers do. In July of 2020, I sat down to write a piece that I have wanted to create for quite some time. I wanted to capture the entire, painful metamorphosis of a journey that was my life during the last two years.

The long, narrative poem on the following pages metaphorically details that segment of my life, in all its "ugly" and its "glory". In it, there is pain, loss, grief, heartache, darkness, strength, power, and healing.

Completing the final line felt like the first deep breath I had taken in years.

In it, I hope you find a bit of yourself. I hope you find a bit of hope. Thank you, my readers, for allowing my words into your hearts.

"Chrysalis"

I rubbed the ashes
of the life I used to live
into the pores of my skin,
hoping they'd absorb the history
now lost to me.
But they didn't listen.
So, I dug the soles of my feet;
careworn and weary,
into the dirt path
that last led me home,
all I found was a different road.
So, I pictured myself a sail,
and beckoned the winds
to point me in the right direction.
but they held me still,
and claimed it was for my own protection.

Rooted firmly into place,
nothing to run from,
nothing left to chase,
in a strange land; no plans...
no tricks left up my torn sleeves;
threadbare at the seams of me.
I could do nothing except
to bless the ground with my collapse.
I couldn't frame the synapses
to bring back what had gone,
because I'd never been more alone,
and emptiness ripples the surface of the storm,
like tears from a dripping faucet,
or loss that sinks in slow;
a stone settling in your chest.

Loneliness carries an echo;
on and on.

I began to turn to stone.
Time ticked by as the earth spun around me.
Somewhere outside of the confines of gravity,
everything was changing... except me.
Soundlessly, I existed between the whistles in the breeze,
and the rustling of autumn leaves;
golden like the edges of blurred memories;
old Polaroids in a box under the bed; collecting dust.
Everything tasted like blood and looked like rust.
The weight of the world blew out my knees;
a broken creature of a dead routine.
An end result; a byproduct,
decaying.

Please, a moment; anything-
just let me gather my strength.
can't anything remain?

My body, my being;
heavy,
hardening,
melted into the shell
now surrounding me.
I longed for four walls
and a compass,
with the needle spinning.

If I alone
had built my prison;
this cocoon inside my mind,
surely I could break it
(couldn't I?)
I knew I had to try,
or I would die inside myself;
sleeping in a blind spot,
carrion for vultures circling;
a carcass left to rot.
Only exposed bones picked clean,
scattered in the wind; indifferent
would ever be left of me then.

I needed to get out.

So, I harnessed the raw power
of every piece of grief,
of every love I'd lost,
of every price
for which I'd paid
far too high a cost...
and I raised my shaking fist
Shale splintering rock
into whatever comes next...

I broke through my own encasement,
somewhere adjacent to stubbornness.

I learned that trauma
has to travel with us;
old luggage without a tag,
worn leather, faded; scratched.
But we can put it on our backs
when our arms give out.

I once pictured my life so loud
but wisdom whispers; never screams...

Fortitude is something
that we must unearth.
Hiding is something
that we must unlearn.
Thus, I emerged; caked in dirt.

My eyes clearing,
my hands machetes;
finally ready to cut aside
anything that would impede
the road in front of me.

Fear is a rest stop
on the long road
to discovery,
and I have to make good time...
where am I?

I considered the road again;
resolute but directionless,
and wept
for the pain and beauty
of new possibility.

One foot in front of the other;
tentatively walking,
joints and bones talking
in cracks and pops and creaks,
to the nervous muscles I was again using.

Moving parts grinding to slow life,
sleepless nights giving way to fight.
And that made all the difference
to once-blind eyes re-learning to see;
a new path unfolding before me.

Standing, I shed my former armor,
summoning the courage to go softly.

In the end,
all that's left is this...

It's all in the trying.

Finally;

an ocean of pain
and the past
behind me,
in the rearview,
with a clear view ahead.

Moving.

Healing.

Free.

Ready to live again.

The ringing of my own laughter
sounds like the home
I used to know.

And the way forward
is paved with grains of hope
and the promise
(no longer the fear)
of the unknown.

Chrysalis

"Poetry is when an emotion has found its thought and the thought has found words."

-*Robert Frost*

Acknowledgements

Thank you **to Rebecca Connell** for the beautiful cover art and chapter sketches.

Thank you to **Kait Coppock** for designing this beautiful cover.

Thank you to **Kalyani Datta** for the beautiful journal pages.

Thank you to **the talented photographers at Unsplash** for the privilege of using your work to enhance my own.

To my love,

Thank you for believing in and supporting me endlessly.

AFB

About the Author

Stefanie Briar is a wife, mother, English teacher, editor, and poet from southern New Jersey. Writing openly and honestly about pain, love, mental illness, grief, and healing; her work resonates with many.

She has written two other books, "Cosmosis" and "Burn".

She can be found on Instagam @stefanie.briar.poetry, and on TikTok @ stefaniebriarpoetry.

Made in the USA
Middletown, DE
27 December 2022

20438289R00130